Beyond Lemonade Stands: How To Start A Serious Business At 16

Table of Contents

Young Entrepreneur: Unleashing Your Potential   2

Choosing Your Path: Identifying a Profitable Business   5

Building a Solid Foundation: Crafting a Business Plan   11

Financial Savvy: Funding and Managing Your Business Finances   15

Making Your Mark: Effective Branding and Marketing Strategies   20

Navigating Legal Landscapes: Ensuring Your Business Operates Within the Law   24

Inspiring Journeys: Success Stories and Next Steps for Young Entrepreneurs   29

Young Entrepreneur: Unleashing Your Potential

Every successful business journey begins with the realization of one's potential, and it's no different for you, the young entrepreneur. As a 16-year-old, you possess an extraordinary mix of passion, energy, creativity, and time, all of which can fuel your entrepreneurial journey. The aim of this chapter is to help you understand, recognize, and unleash that potential.

Understanding Your Potential

Potential is the inherent ability or capacity for growth, development, or future success. It's like a seed buried in the soil, awaiting the right conditions to sprout and flourish. For young entrepreneurs, your potential is your natural talent, skills, creativity, passion, and most importantly, your capacity to learn and adapt.

Understanding your potential involves honest introspection. Start by asking yourself: What am I good at? What do I enjoy doing? What are my interests and passions? Do others commend me for certain skills or talents? Reflect on these questions and make a list of your strengths and passions. They form the foundation of your entrepreneurial potential.

Unleashing Your Potential

Unleashing your potential involves refining these innate abilities, then leveraging them in pursuit of your entrepreneurial goals. Let's explore how to do this:

Develop Your Skills: Your strengths provide a starting point, but skills development is a continuous process. Identify resources that can help you improve these skills. Online courses, books, podcasts, or mentorships can all be effective ways to learn and grow. If you're good at coding, for example, engage in more complex projects or learn new programming languages. If you're skilled at art, explore different mediums and styles.

Fuel Your Passion: The most successful entrepreneurs are often those who turn their passions into a business. Passion fuels perseverance, a critical quality for any entrepreneur. If you love what you're doing, you'll be willing to put in the time and effort, even when challenges arise. For example, if you love baking, consider a business centered around that.

Embrace Creativity and Innovation: As a young entrepreneur, one of your greatest advantages is your fresh perspective. You can look at existing problems and see solutions that others might miss. Don't be afraid to think outside the box. Innovative ideas are often the basis of successful businesses.

Cultivate a Growth Mindset: A growth mindset is the belief that abilities and intelligence can be developed over time. Embracing this mindset means viewing challenges as opportunities for learning, not as insurmountable obstacles. It also means understanding that failure is a part of the entrepreneurial journey, providing valuable lessons that can propel you towards success.

Set Clear Goals: Having a clear vision of what you want to achieve is crucial. Your goals should be specific, measurable, attainable, relevant, and time-bound (SMART). Goals give you a direction and help you track your progress. For instance, a goal could be to launch your online bakery business by the end of the school year.

Network: Build relationships with like-minded peers, mentors, and industry professionals. Networking can open doors to opportunities and collaborations that can accelerate your entrepreneurial journey.

As a young entrepreneur, your potential is immense. It's a powerful blend of talent, skills, passion, creativity, and the ability to learn and adapt. Recognizing and unleashing this potential is the first step towards your entrepreneurial success.

In this digital age, you have more resources at your disposal than any generation before. Online courses, digital tools, and social platforms provide unprecedented opportunities for learning, networking, and marketing. Leverage these tools to enhance your skills, refine your ideas, and build your brand.

However, remember that being an entrepreneur isn't just about building a successful business. It's about personal growth, resilience, and making a positive impact. As you embark on this journey, embrace the challenges and failures as opportunities for learning and growth. Believe in your potential, stay focused on your goals, and you'll be well on your way to building a serious business at 16.

In the next chapter, we'll delve into how to choose the right business for you. We'll explore various profitable business options for young entrepreneurs, along with the factors you should consider in making your decision. But remember, your business idea should not only be profitable, but it should also be something you're passionate about.

Choosing Your Path: Identifying a Profitable Business

Having a clear understanding of your potential as an entrepreneur is the first step towards building a successful business. The next step is to decide which path to take — that is, identifying a profitable business that aligns with your interests and skills. This chapter will provide a comprehensive guide on how to go about selecting the right business venture for you.

Understanding Your Market

Before diving into specific business ideas, it's crucial to understand the concept of the 'market' and why it's an important factor in your decision-making process.

In simple terms, a market is a place where buyers and sellers interact to exchange goods or services. Each market has its unique characteristics, including the size (number of potential customers), growth potential, competition, and customer needs and preferences.

Understanding your market involves conducting market research. This could include:

1. **Identifying Your Target Customers:** Who are the people that would be interested in your product or service? What are their demographics (age, gender, location, etc.)? What are their preferences and needs?

2. **Analyzing Your Competition:** Who else is providing similar products or services? What are their strengths and weaknesses? What can you do differently or better?

3. **Assessing Market Size and Growth:** How many potential customers are there for your product or service? Is this market growing, stable, or declining?

4. **Identifying Trends:** Are there any trends in the market that you could take advantage of? For instance, there's currently a trend towards healthier and more sustainable products.

Selecting a Business Idea

Now that you have a grasp of what a market is and the importance of understanding it, let's delve into the process of selecting a profitable business idea. Here are some steps to guide you:

1. **Align with Your Interests and Skills:** As mentioned in Chapter 1, the most successful entrepreneurs often turn their passions into a business. List down your hobbies, skills, and interests, then brainstorm business ideas that align with them.

2. **Identify Problems to Solve:** Great business ideas often come from solving problems. Think about the problems you, your family, or your community face. Can you create a product or service that solves these problems?

3. **Look for Gaps in the Market:** Sometimes, customers might be looking for a specific product or service that isn't available or

doesn't meet their expectations. Identifying these gaps and filling them is another way to come up with a business idea.

4. **Evaluate Your Ideas:** Once you have a list of potential business ideas, evaluate them based on their market potential (using the market research methods discussed earlier), the required startup capital, and how passionate you are about the idea.

5. **Test Your Idea:** Before fully launching your business, it's advisable to test your idea on a small scale. This could involve creating a prototype of your product and getting feedback, or launching a mini version of your service to see how it's received.

Some Profitable Business Ideas for Young Entrepreneurs

To get your brainstorming started, here are some profitable business ideas that young entrepreneurs like you have pursued:

1. **Online Reselling**: With the rise of e-commerce platforms, buying and reselling items online has become a lucrative business. You could resell anything from vintage clothing to collectibles. Your unique perspective as a young person can help you identify trendy products that will sell well among your peers.

2. **Tutoring**: If you're particularly good at a certain subject, you can offer tutoring services to other students. This could be done in person or online.

3. **Graphic Design Services**: If you have a knack for design, you can start a graphic design business. Many businesses need

logos, flyers, social media graphics, and other designs.

4. **Social Media Consultancy**: Many small businesses need help managing their social media presence. If you're savvy with platforms like Instagram, TikTok, or Twitter, you can offer social media consultancy services.

5. **Crafts or Handmade Products**: If you're good with your hands, you can start a business selling handmade products. This could be jewelry, soap, candles, or any other craft.

6. **Pet Services**: If you love animals, you could start a pet sitting, dog walking, or pet grooming business.

7. **Mobile Applications**: If you're tech-savvy and have a great idea for an app, this could be a highly profitable venture.

Remember, these are just examples. The best business idea for you will depend on your unique skills, interests, and the needs of your market.

Choosing a business is a critical step in your entrepreneurial journey. It requires self-reflection, brainstorming, market research, evaluation, and testing. The most profitable business for you will align with your interests and skills, solve a problem or meet a need in the market, and have growth potential.

As you go through this process, remember to keep an open mind. Sometimes, the most successful businesses come from the most unexpected ideas. Don't be afraid to think outside the box and push the boundaries.

In the next chapter, we'll explore how to turn your business idea into a concrete plan. This will involve setting your business goals, defining your strategies, and planning your operations, among other things.

Choosing your path might not be a straightforward or easy process, but it's a thrilling one. It's the process where your business starts to take shape. As you embark on this journey, remember to trust your instincts, embrace the learning process, and enjoy the ride. After all, as a young entrepreneur, you're not just building a business – you're building your future.

Building a Solid Foundation: Crafting a Business Plan

Identifying a profitable business that aligns with your skills and interests is an exciting milestone in your entrepreneurial journey. But it's only the beginning. To transform this idea into a successful business, you need a robust plan. The aim of this chapter is to guide you on how to craft a comprehensive business plan that will serve as a blueprint for your entrepreneurial journey.

Understanding the Importance of a Business Plan

A business plan is a written document that details what your business is, what it aims to achieve, and how it will achieve it. It serves multiple purposes:

1. **Roadmap:** A business plan provides a roadmap for your business, outlining your goals and the steps you need to take to achieve them. It's a guide that helps you stay on track and make informed decisions.

2. **Feasibility Test:** Writing a business plan forces you to evaluate the feasibility of your business idea. You'll need to research your market, analyse your competition, and forecast your finances, giving you a realistic view of whether your business can succeed.

3. **Funding Tool:** If you need to seek funding from investors or lenders, a well-written business plan can showcase the potential of your business and convince them to invest.

Crafting Your Business Plan

A comprehensive business plan includes several sections. Each section serves a particular purpose and contributes to the overall picture of your business.

1. **Executive Summary:** This is a brief overview of your business plan, summarizing your business and its goals. Although it's the first section of your plan, it's usually written last, after you've fleshed out the details in the other sections.

2. **Company Description:** This section provides detailed information about your business. What type of business is it? What products or services does it offer? What problem does it solve, or what need does it meet?

3. **Market Analysis:** Here, you'll present the findings from your market research. This includes information about your target customers, your competition, and the overall state and trends of your market.

4. **Organization and Management:** This section outlines your business's organizational structure and management team. As a

sole proprietor, this could just be you. But if you have a partner or employees, you'll need to detail their roles.

5. **Services or Products:** Here, you'll describe what you're selling. What are the benefits of your products or services? How do they meet the needs of your target customers?

6. **Marketing and Sales Strategy:** This section outlines how you'll attract and retain customers. This includes your branding strategy, pricing strategy, advertising and promotion strategies, and sales strategy.

7. **Funding Request (if applicable):** If you're seeking funding, this section details how much you need, how you'll use the funds, and your plans for repaying any loans.

8. **Financial Projections:** This section provides a forecast of your business's financial future. This includes projected income statements, balance sheets, and cash flow statements. You'll need to justify your projections based on your market analysis and marketing strategy.

9. **Appendix (if applicable):** An appendix includes any supporting documents or additional information that complements your business plan.

Remember, your business plan is not set in stone. It's a living document that should evolve with your business. As your business grows and the market changes, you'll need to revisit and revise your business plan to reflect these changes.

Conclusion

A solid business plan is the foundation of a successful business. It provides a roadmap for your business, tests the feasibility of your idea, and can help you secure funding. Crafting a comprehensive business plan requires careful thought, research, and planning, but the effort you put in will pay off in the long run.

In the next chapter, we'll delve into how to fund your business. We'll explore different funding options for young entrepreneurs, along with the pros and cons of each, and provide guidance on how to approach potential investors or lenders.

Crafting a business plan might seem daunting, especially at the age of 16. But remember, every successful entrepreneur started somewhere. By taking the time to plan your business, you're not just planning for success – you're planning for sustainable, long-term growth. So, embrace the process, and take one step at a time. You're building the foundation of your entrepreneurial dream.

Financial Savvy: Funding and Managing Your Business Finances

Starting a business often requires some level of financial investment. Depending on your business model, you might need funds to buy equipment, purchase inventory, set up a website, or hire employees. How you source and manage this capital is crucial to the survival and growth of your business. This chapter provides an in-depth guide on how to finance your business and manage your finances effectively.

Understanding Your Financing Needs

Before exploring various financing options, you need to understand your financing needs. This involves estimating the costs of starting and running your business. Remember that it's always better to overestimate your costs to avoid running out of funds.

Your startup costs will depend on your business model. They might include:

- Equipment or machinery
- Inventory
- Business registration and licenses
- Website and e-commerce setup
- Advertising and promotion

- Insurance
- Rent and utilities (if you have a physical location)
- Professional services (e.g., legal or accounting services)

Once you've estimated your startup costs, you need to forecast your operating costs. These are the costs of running your business on a day-to-day basis, such as:

- Raw materials or inventory
- Packaging and shipping costs
- Employee wages (if applicable)
- Rent and utilities
- Website hosting and maintenance
- Advertising and marketing
- Taxes
- Insurance

Your financial projections from your business plan should provide a comprehensive estimate of these costs.

Exploring Financing Options

Now that you understand your financing needs let's explore some financing options for young entrepreneurs:

1. **Personal Savings:** Many entrepreneurs start their businesses using their savings. This is often the easiest and most

straightforward way to finance a business, and it doesn't involve paying interest or giving up equity.

2. **Family and Friends:** Sometimes, family and friends who believe in your business idea might be willing to lend you money or invest in your business.

3. **Crowdfunding:** Crowdfunding involves raising small amounts of money from a large number of people, typically via the internet. You could offer a product, a share in your business, or a simple thank you in return for their contribution.

4. **Grants and Competitions:** Some organizations and institutions offer grants or run competitions to support young entrepreneurs. These could provide you with startup funds that you don't need to repay.

5. **Angel Investors and Venture Capitalists:** Angel investors and venture capitalists are individuals or firms that invest in businesses for a share of the equity. While it's less common for young entrepreneurs to secure this type of funding, it's not impossible, especially if you have a highly innovative and scalable business idea.

6. **Loans:** Some banks and financial institutions offer loans to small businesses. However, you'll typically need a solid business plan and possibly some collateral to secure a loan.

Each financing option has its pros and cons, and the best one for you will depend on your specific circumstances.

Managing Your Business Finances

Securing financing is just the first step. It's equally important to manage your business finances effectively. Here are some key aspects of financial management:

1. **Budgeting**: Based on your financial projections, create a budget for your business. This should outline your expected income and expenses, helping you plan for the future and avoid overspending.

2. **Accounting**: Keep track of all your income and expenses. This will help you monitor your business's financial performance, make informed decisions, and fulfill your tax obligations.

3. **Cash Flow Management**: Cash flow is the money that flows in and out of your business. You need to ensure that you always have enough cash to cover your expenses. This could involve managing your inventory effectively, offering or seeking credit terms, and controlling your costs.

4. **Taxes**: Understand your tax obligations and plan for them. Depending on your business structure and location, you might need to pay income tax, sales tax, or other types of tax. You might

want to seek advice from a tax professional to ensure you comply with all tax laws.

5. **Insurance:** Protect your business from potential risks by getting the right insurance. This could include liability insurance, property insurance, or workers' compensation insurance, depending on your business.

Financing your business and managing your finances are crucial aspects of your entrepreneurial journey. It involves planning, making informed decisions, and ongoing management. Don't be afraid to seek help or advice, whether from a mentor, a financial advisor, or educational resources.

In the next chapter, we'll discuss how to create a compelling brand and market your business. We'll delve into the concepts of branding, marketing strategies, and customer relationship management.

Managing your business finances might seem daunting, especially if you're new to the world of business. But remember, financial management is a skill that can be learned. By taking the time to understand your financing needs, explore financing options, and manage your finances effectively, you're building the financial foundation of your entrepreneurial dream. So, embrace the learning process, and take one step at a time. You're not just building a business – you're building your future.

Making Your Mark: Effective Branding and Marketing Strategies

A great business idea, solid financial planning, and a robust business plan are crucial to the success of your entrepreneurial journey. Still, without a compelling brand and effective marketing strategies, your business might struggle to attract and retain customers. This chapter is designed to provide a comprehensive guide on how to create a compelling brand and develop effective marketing strategies for your business.

The Power of a Strong Brand

At its core, your brand is the identity of your business. It's how your business is perceived by the world. It includes your business name, logo, color scheme, and tone of voice, but it's also more than that. It's your values, your mission, and the experience you promise to your customers.

A strong brand can:

- **Differentiate you from competitors:** In a crowded market, a strong brand can help your business stand out and be memorable.

- **Build customer loyalty:** If customers have a positive experience with your brand, they're more likely to stay loyal and recommend your business to others.
- **Add value to your business:** A strong brand can command higher prices and attract investors or buyers.

Crafting Your Brand

Creating a brand for your business involves several steps:

1. **Define your brand identity:** This includes your mission (why your business exists), your values (what principles guide your business), your brand personality (if your brand was a person, what would it be like?), and your unique selling proposition (what sets your business apart?).

2. **Choose your business name:** Your business name is a crucial part of your brand. It should reflect your brand identity, be easy to pronounce and remember, and be unique.

3. **Design your logo and visual elements:** Your logo is often the first thing people notice about your brand. It should be simple, memorable, and representative of your brand identity. Other visual elements of your brand include your color scheme, typography, and any other design elements.

4. **Develop your brand voice:** Your brand voice is how your brand "speaks" in all its communications, including your website, social media posts, emails, and advertisements. It should reflect your brand personality and resonate with your target customers.

Unveiling Your Brand

Once you've created your brand, you need to introduce it to the world. This involves incorporating your branding into every aspect of your business, including your website, social media profiles, packaging, customer service, and even your business operations.

Developing Your Marketing Strategies

Now that you've created a compelling brand, you need to market your business. Marketing involves promoting your business and its products or services to attract and retain customers.

Here are some key steps to developing your marketing strategies:

1. **Understand your target market:** You can't effectively market your business without understanding who your customers are. You need to know their demographics, their needs and wants, and where they hang out, both online and offline.

2. **Define your marketing goals:** Your marketing goals could include increasing brand awareness, attracting new customers, retaining existing customers, or increasing sales. Your goals should align with your overall business goals.

3. **Choose your marketing channels:** Based on your target market, choose the most effective channels to reach your customers. This could include social media, email marketing, content marketing (such as blogs or videos), search engine optimization (SEO), pay-per-click (PPC) advertising, or traditional marketing methods like print ads or events.

4. **Develop your marketing campaigns:** A marketing campaign is a coordinated series of steps to promote your business or a particular product or service. Each campaign should have a specific goal, a target audience, a chosen marketing channel, and a way to measure success.

5. **Measure and adjust:** Marketing is not a set-and-forget task. You need to measure the effectiveness of your marketing strategies and adjust them based on the results. You might need to try different strategies or tweak your existing ones to find what works best for your business.

Building a compelling brand and developing effective marketing strategies are crucial to attracting and retaining customers. This involves understanding your brand identity, crafting your brand, unveiling it to the world, understanding your target market, defining your marketing goals, choosing your marketing channels, developing your marketing campaigns, and constantly measuring and adjusting your strategies.

In the next chapter, we'll discuss how to navigate the legal landscape of starting a business. We'll delve into the concepts of business structure, licenses and permits, intellectual property, and legal obligations.

Creating a brand and marketing your business might seem daunting, especially if you're new to the world of business. But remember, branding and marketing are skills that can be learned. By taking the time to understand your brand, develop your marketing strategies, and learn from your results, you're not just building a business – you're building a legacy. So, embrace the learning process, and take one step at a time. You're not just making your mark in the business world – you're making your mark in the world.

Navigating Legal Landscapes: Ensuring Your Business Operates Within the Law

Setting up a business goes beyond developing an idea and launching a product or service. It also involves understanding and complying with a myriad of legal obligations. The legal landscape of starting a business can be complex and might seem intimidating, but it is a crucial aspect that can protect your business in the long term. This chapter is designed to provide a comprehensive guide on the legal aspects of starting a business, focusing on business structure, licenses and permits, intellectual property, and other legal obligations.

Choosing the Right Business Structure

The structure of your business significantly impacts various aspects such as taxation, liability, and control over the company. The common types of business structures include:

1. **Sole Proprietorship:** This is the simplest structure, where the business is entirely owned and controlled by a single individual, who is responsible for all assets and liabilities.

2. **Partnership:** This structure involves two or more individuals who agree to share the profits or losses of a business.

3. **Limited Liability Company (LLC):** This structure combines elements of partnerships and corporations, offering owners protection from personal liability while providing flexibility in operation.

4. **Corporation:** This is a more complex structure where the business is a separate legal entity owned by shareholders.

Each structure has its pros and cons, and it's crucial to consider factors like the nature of your business, your financial situation, and your future plans before making a decision. It may also be beneficial to consult with a legal professional to choose the right structure for your business.

Understanding Licenses and Permits

Depending on the nature of your business and where it's located, you may need certain licenses and permits to operate legally. These can range from a general business license to specific permits for activities like selling food or alcohol, or providing certain professional services. Be sure to research the licensing requirements in your city, state, and country, and apply for all necessary licenses and permits well before you plan to start operating.

Protecting Your Intellectual Property

Intellectual property (IP) refers to creations of the mind, such as inventions, literary and artistic works, designs, and symbols, names, and images used in commerce. IP is protected by law through patents, copyright, and trademarks, allowing individuals or businesses to earn recognition or financial benefits from their inventions or creations:

1. **Patents:** A patent is an exclusive right granted for an invention. It provides the patent owner with the right to decide how - or whether - the invention can be used by others.

2. **Copyright:** This is a legal term used to describe the rights that creators have over their literary and artistic works.

3. **Trademarks:** A trademark is a sign capable of distinguishing the goods or services of one enterprise from those of other enterprises.

If your business involves creating and using intellectual property, it's crucial to understand and use IP law to protect your creations and your brand.

Navigating Other Legal Obligations

Apart from the above, there are other legal aspects you should consider, such as:

1. **Employment Laws:** If you plan to hire employees, you'll need to understand the laws related to wages, work hours, safety compliance, and discrimination.

2. **Privacy Laws:** If your business collects personal data from customers (such as names, email addresses, or credit card information), you need to understand and comply with privacy laws.

3. **Tax Laws:** Your business structure, location, and operations will determine what taxes your business has to pay. You may need to register for certain state and federal taxes.

4. **Contract Laws:** Contracts are a fundamental part of doing business. Understanding contract laws can help you create and review contracts more effectively.

Understanding the legal landscape and ensuring compliance is crucial in setting a solid foundation for your business. While the legal aspects of starting a business might seem daunting, they're not insurmountable. With due diligence, research, and perhaps some professional legal advice, you can confidently navigate these legal waters. In the next chapter, we will explore another crucial aspect of business – financial management. From funding your business to managing cash flow, we will delve into how you can effectively handle the financial side of your business. Remember, starting a business is not just about turning a profit; it's about doing so responsibly and legally. This way, you protect your business, your customers, and yourself.

Inspiring Journeys: Success Stories and Next Steps for Young Entrepreneurs

As we have walked through the process of identifying a business idea, crafting a solid business plan, managing finances, and navigating legal landscapes, it's now time to seek inspiration from those who have walked the path before us and successfully charted their course in the entrepreneurial world. Moreover, we will explore practical next steps to embolden you on your journey as a young entrepreneur.

Success Stories of Young Entrepreneurs

1. **Mark Zuckerberg – Facebook:** Perhaps one of the most famous young entrepreneurs, Mark Zuckerberg co-founded Facebook at 19 while studying at Harvard. Facebook revolutionized the way we connect with people worldwide and became one of the most successful tech companies globally.

2. **Mikaila Ulmer – Me & the Bees Lemonade:** At just 4 years old, Mikaila Ulmer started Me & the Bees Lemonade based on her grandmother's flaxseed lemonade recipe. Today, her product is sold in major supermarket chains, and Mikaila is a sought-after speaker on entrepreneurship and bees' protection.

3. **Nick D'Aloisio – Summly:** At 15, Nick D'Aloisio created Summly, an app that summarizes news articles, which was later

acquired by Yahoo for approximately $30 million. D'Aloisio's journey demonstrates how innovation can pave the way to success at a young age.

4. **Ritesh Agarwal – OYO Rooms:** Ritesh Agarwal started OYO Rooms at the age of 19. OYO Rooms is a network of budget hotels in India, and Agarwal's dedication and unique business model led the company to massive success, making him one of India's youngest billionaires.

These are just a few of many inspiring young entrepreneurs who turned their innovative ideas into successful businesses. These stories emphasize that age is not a barrier to success in entrepreneurship.

Next Steps for Young Entrepreneurs

1. **Keep Learning:** No matter how much you know, there's always more to learn. Stay curious about new business trends, changes in your industry, and potential areas for your personal and professional development.

2. **Network:** Surround yourself with other entrepreneurs and professionals. Attend networking events, join online communities, and consider finding a mentor.

3. **Refine Your Business Plan:** Your business plan is a living document. As you learn and grow, and as your business evolves, keep refining your business plan to reflect these changes.

4. **Seek Feedback and Improve:** Whether it's from customers, mentors, or team members, seek feedback regularly and use it to improve your products, services, and business processes.

5. **Prioritize Your Well-being:** Entrepreneurship can be demanding, so it's essential to take care of your physical, mental, and emotional well-being. Set boundaries, take time for self-care, and don't neglect your hobbies and personal interests.

Becoming an entrepreneur at a young age can be an exciting and rewarding journey. It allows you to bring your ideas to life, make a difference, and build a fulfilling career. But it's also a journey that requires passion, resilience, and continual learning. Remember the success stories of young entrepreneurs who have walked this path before you – they faced challenges, learned, adapted, and succeeded.

You have taken the first steps by learning about starting a business. Now it's time to take action. Continue learning, stay motivated, and believe in your ability to create a successful business. The entrepreneurial journey is not always smooth sailing, but with determination, creativity, and hard work, you can navigate the path to success. This is just the beginning of your journey.

Now, let's see where it takes you.

www.ingramcontent.com/pod-product-compliance
Lightning Source LLC
Chambersburg PA
CBHW031516210526
45464CB00007B/2940